FAR-OUT GUIDE TO

NEPTUNE

FAR-OUT GUIDE
to the
SOLAR SYSTEM

Mary Kay Carson

Bailey Books
an imprint of
Enslow Publishers, Inc.
40 Industrial Road
Box 398
Berkeley Heights, NJ 07922
USA
http://www.enslow.com

For Christopher Phillip Fry

Bailey Books, an imprint of Enslow Publishers, Inc.

Library of Congress Cataloging-in-Publication Data

Carson, Mary Kay.
    Far-out guide to Neptune / Mary Kay Carson.
        p. cm. — (Far-out guide to the solar system)
    Includes bibliographical references and index.
    Summary: "Presents information about Neptune, including fast facts, history, and technology used to study the planet"—Provided by publisher.
    ISBN 978-0-7660-3186-9 (Library Ed.)
    ISBN 978-1-59845-189-4 (Paperback Ed.)
    1. Neptune (Planet)—Juvenile literature. 2. Solar system—Juvenile literature. I. Title.
    QB691.C37 2011
    523.48—dc22
                         2008050037

Printed in China

052010 Leo Paper Group, Heshan City, Guangdong, China

10 9 8 7 6 5 4 3 2 1

To Our Readers: We have done our best to make sure all Internet Addresses in this book were active and appropriate when we went to press. However, the author and the publisher have no control over and assume no liability for the material available on those Internet sites or on other Web sites they may link to. Any comments or suggestions can be sent by e-mail to comments@enslow.com or to the address on the back cover.

Image Credits: Boeing Satellite Systems, p. 43; Enslow Publishers, Inc., p. 9; JPL, p. 17; Lunar and Planetary Institute, pp. 1, 6, 7 (right); NASA, pp. 3, 7 (left), 12, 25, 32, 34 (top), 38; NASA and STScI, p. 19; NASA, ESA, E. Karkoschka (University of Arizona), and H.B. Hammel (Space Science Institute, Boulder, Colorado), p. 23; NASA, L. Sromovsky, and P. Fry (University of Wisconsin–Madison), p. 22; NASA/JPL, pp. 1, 4–5, 11, 13, 15, 30, 34 (bottom), 40–41; Rendering by Craig Agnor, p. 37.

Cover Image: Lunar and Planetary Institute and NASA/JPL.

Cover illustration shows Voyager 2 *and Neptune.*

CONTENTS

INTRODUCTION
5

CHAPTER 1
WATCHING WILD WEATHER
10

NEPTUNE AT A GLANCE
25

FAST FACTS ABOUT NEPTUNE
26

NEPTUNE TIMELINE OF
EXPLORATION AND DISCOVERY
29

CHAPTER 2
ODDBALL TRITON
31

CHAPTER 3
WHAT'S NEXT FOR NEPTUNE?
40

WORDS TO KNOW
44

FIND OUT MORE AND GET UPDATES
46

INDEX
48

NEPTUNE is the eighth planet from the Sun. (Note that the planets' distances are not shown to scale.)

INTRODUCTION

Did you know that Neptune has rings? Unlike Saturn's famous rings, Neptune's are faint and hard to see. How do we know about the rings? Astronomers used telescopes to get a first peek at them in the mid-1980s. The rings came into view when Neptune passed in front of a star that lit up the rings from behind. You will learn lots more far-out facts about Neptune in this book. Just keep reading!

Neptune is the farthest planet from the Sun. How far is this far-off world? A car ride there from Earth would take more than 5,000 years. Of course, a car cannot travel through space. Nor could a car drive around on Neptune, because there is nothing solid to drive on.

NEPTUNE VS. PLUTO

Neptune has not always been the farthest planet from the Sun. Pluto was discovered in 1930 and called a planet until 2006. (Now Pluto is one of several dwarf planets in our solar system.) For most of those 76 years, Pluto was the farthest planet. But from 1979 to 1999, Neptune was farther from the Sun than Pluto because of Pluto's slanted orbit. Pluto loops inside Neptune's orbit a bit. For 20 years of Pluto's 248-year orbit, Neptune is farther from the Sun than Pluto! It will happen again from 2226 to 2246.

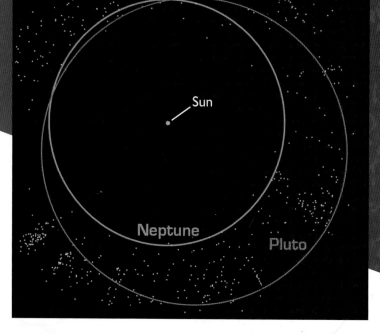

Sun

Neptune

Pluto

NOTICE Pluto's slanted orbit. It takes the dwarf planet inside Neptune's path during part of its journey around the Sun.

Neptune is a landless gas giant. Like Jupiter, Saturn, and Uranus, it is a gas and liquid world.

Not much sunlight reaches Neptune. Being so far from the Sun makes it a cold, dark place. But Neptune is a planet full of surprises. Where are the fastest winds in the solar system? Neptune. Where do giant swirling storms suddenly appear and disappear? Neptune. Even its beautiful bright blue color is surprising. Does your kitchen's stove use natural gas, or methane? Methane makes both Uranus and Neptune bluish. No one knows why Neptune is a brighter blue—at least not yet.

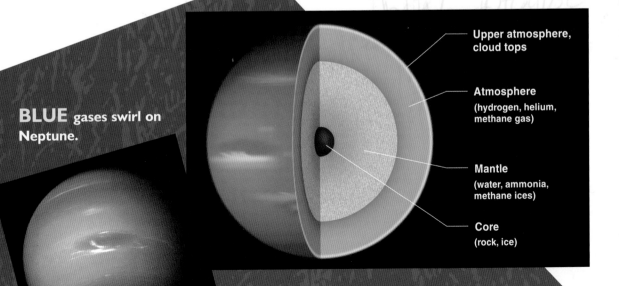

BLUE gases swirl on Neptune.

Upper atmosphere, cloud tops

Atmosphere
(hydrogen, helium, methane gas)

Mantle
(water, ammonia, methane ices)

Core
(rock, ice)

NEPTUNE has a thick atmosphere of gases, with liquid underneath. Scientists think it has a solid core of rock and ice.

PLANETARY MATH PROBLEM

Even Neptune's discovery was surprising. No one simply spotted it with a telescope, the way William Herschel found Uranus in 1781. Neptune was found by solving a math problem. It's true! Math discovered the eighth planet.

Mercury, Venus, Mars, Jupiter, and Saturn can all be seen with the naked eye. People have known about them for thousands of years. Uranus's discovery was a big deal because it was the first planet ever discovered by telescope. Soon everyone was tracking Uranus's orbit. That is where the math problem came in. Uranus's path around the Sun did not make sense. Some years the new planet raced ahead on its path, while other years it dragged behind.

What could be wrong with the seventh planet's orbit? By the 1830s, astronomers had it figured out. They believed that an eighth planet's gravity was tugging at Uranus, causing its irregular orbit. No one had seen a planet beyond Uranus, but they could do the math. By 1846, two different men had solved Uranus's orbit mystery. They both predicted an eighth planet about

1.5 billion kilometers (1 billion miles) past Uranus. This position would cause Uranus's irregular path. And they were right. Once astronomers knew where to look, they quickly found Neptune. It was spotted with a telescope in the fall of 1846. They found the eighth planet exactly where the math said it would be.

FAR-OUT FACT

NEPTUNE'S INTERNATIONAL DISCOVERERS CLUB

English astronomer John Couch Adams was the first to solve the planetary math problem in 1845, but no one took him seriously enough to start looking for an eighth planet. Meanwhile Urbain J.J. Le Verrier figured it out, too, and told some astronomers where to look. On September 23, 1846, German astronomer Johann Galle used Le Verrier's predictions to find an eighth planet. The discoverers agreed to name the new planet after the Roman god of the deep blue sea, Neptune.

NEPTUNE'S discovery is often credited to these three men: John C. Adams (left), Urbain J.J. Le Verrier (center), and Johann Galle (right).

CHAPTER 1

WATCHING WILD WEATHER

More than 160 years have passed since Neptune's discovery. But the farthest planet still holds many surprises. "The thing I love about Neptune is that I never know what I'm going to see when I go to the telescope," said Heidi Hammel. Hammel is an expert on Neptune. She has spent her whole career studying it.

Carsickness got Hammel started stargazing. Riding in the car on family trips as a kid made her feel terrible. "I had to lie on the backseat

NEPTUNE'S ever-changing atmosphere swirls and streaks with stormy methane clouds.

PLANETARY astronomer
Heidi Hammel is a Neptune
expert.

being sick," explained Hammel. "[A]nd the only thing I
could do was look out the window and see the stars." So
young Hammel passed the time learning star names. She
grew up to become a planetary astronomer. When she was
in college, telescopes were the only way to study Neptune,

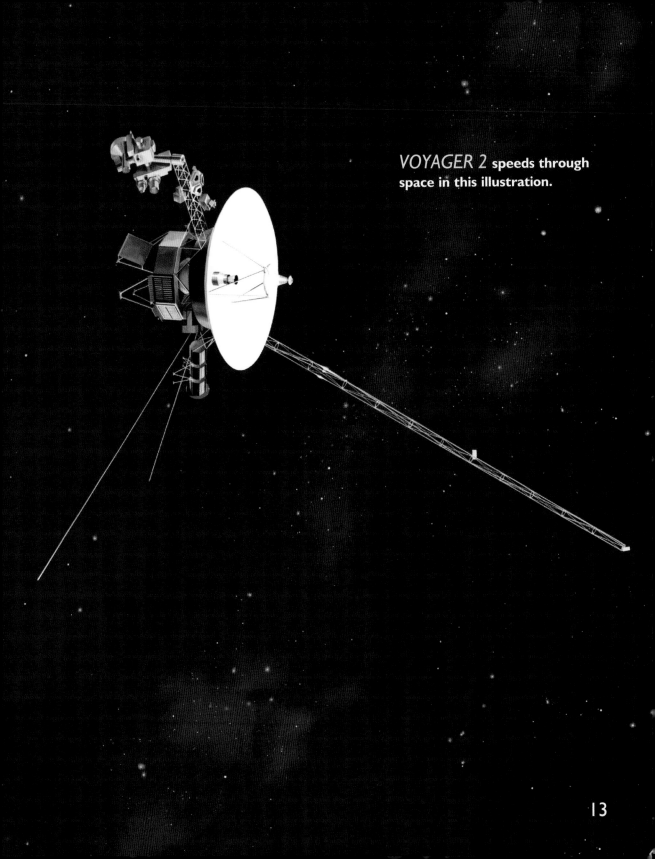

VOYAGER 2 speeds through space in this illustration.

so that is how Hammel watched its wild weather and blue clouds. In 1989, a spacecraft neared Neptune. It would get the first ever close-up look at the distant planet. What would *Voyager 2* see?

NEPTUNE UP CLOSE

Voyager 2 blasted off atop a rocket in the summer of 1977. It traveled for 12 years to reach Neptune! *Voyager 2* became the first (and so far only) spacecraft to visit Neptune in August 1989. It flew by Neptune's north

FAR-OUT FACT

VOYAGER 2'S GRAND TOUR

Voyager 1 and *Voyager 2* flew by Jupiter and Saturn between 1979 and 1981. These robotic space probes photographed and studied the two biggest gas giants. Then scientists steered *Voyager 2* on to the smaller gas giants—Uranus and Neptune. The pioneering spacecraft was the first ever to visit Uranus (in 1986) and Neptune (in 1989). Both *Voyagers* are now leaving the solar system, but they will be sending back reports until around 2025.

15

pole at a height of just 4,800 kilometers (3,000 miles). That was closer than it had come to Jupiter, Saturn, or Uranus! Neptune gets very little sunlight, so *Voyager 2* had to shoot pictures in the near dark. Neptune is also very far away. It took four hours for *Voyager 2*'s signals to reach Earth. The amazing space probe successfully snapped and sent back 10,000 pictures.

Voyager 2 discovered six new moons around Neptune and also photographed its rings. The spacecraft found Neptune to be warmer than expected. Strangely, it is not any colder than Uranus, even though it is so much farther from the Sun. *Voyager 2* measured how fast the farthest planet spun. It also recorded the chemical mix of Neptune's atmosphere. *Voyager 2*'s discoveries changed what we know about Neptune—especially what we know about its weather.

Heidi Hammel was a high schooler when *Voyager 2* launched. By the time it neared Neptune, she was an expert on the planet. Hammel was on *Voyager 2*'s science team when the spacecraft visited Neptune. She got an up-close look at its wild weather. Winds raged at 2,000 kilometers (1,200 miles) per hour! Bright white

NEPTUNE'S Great Dark Spot,
photographed by *Voyager 2* in 1989,
is a huge storm.

TELESCOPE IN SPACE

The *Hubble Space Telescope* is both a powerful telescope and an orbiting spacecraft. The space shuttle *Discovery* launched it into space in 1990. Why haul a bus-sized telescope into space? To get above Earth's messy atmosphere, which blurs a ground-based telescope's view. The *Hubble* orbits about 610 kilometers (380 miles) above our planet. Up there the view is very clear. The *Hubble* even has a sharp view of distant galaxies.

clouds zipped around the planet. There were storms, too. "One of the biggest surprises when the *Voyager* spacecraft flew by Neptune was [the image of] a huge dark spot on the planet," said Hammel. The spot was a gigantic storm. *Voyager 2*'s science team named it the Great Dark Spot. Neptune's giant storm was like a hurricane the size of Earth!

Voyager 2's mission to Neptune was an awesome success. While it answered many questions, it brought up a bunch of new ones: Does the planet's weather change?

THE ***Hubble Space Telescope*** **orbits above Earth's blurring atmosphere in this illustration.**

Is Neptune always like this? Do storms like the Great Dark Spot last a long time? Are they rare or common? Answering these kinds of questions meant studying Neptune over time, so astronomers like Hammel went back to their telescopes. Luckily a much better telescope was in the works. It would get a clearer view of the stars— and of planets like Neptune. How? It was going to be out in space.

FAR-OUT FACT

SUNLESS WEATHER

What makes the wind blow or clouds form? On Earth, the Sun controls weather. Its heat evaporates water and creates clouds. Uneven heating of Earth's surface creates wind, too. But what about on Neptune where so little sunlight shines? No one is sure. It probably has something to do with Neptune's warmer-than-expected temperature. There is likely heat deep inside Neptune. When the heat rises toward the dark, cold atmosphere, it stirs up stormy weather.

A CHANGING PLANET

Everybody wants to use the best telescopes. Astronomers often wait years for a turn to use them—especially to use the *Hubble Space Telescope*. Astronomy experts look over about 1,000 requests to use the *Hubble* every year. They can only choose about 200 of them. When Heidi Hammel's first chance to use the *Hubble* came in 1994, she was ready. How did Neptune surprise her this time? The Great Dark Spot was gone! Five years had passed since *Voyager 2* had photographed it. "It had simply disappeared," said Hammel. Then she saw a different big, dark spot on a different part of the planet. No one knew that these giant hurricanes on Neptune could just come and go.

"People have this idea that the farther out you go in the solar system, the colder and slower things are," said Hammel. "They expect Neptune to be dead, but it's one of the most dynamic places we know." Neptune's weather is always changing, just like Earth's weather. Studying storms, clouds, and winds on other planets teaches us about our own planet, too. "That helps us understand

1996

1998

2002

LOOK how much Neptune changed over six years in these *Hubble* photographs! The 2002 picture shows a brighter springtime southern hemisphere.

THE *Hubble* can show us different views of Neptune. The left picture is Neptune's natural color. The enhanced color picture (top right) highlights Neptune's clouds. The methane band (lower right, in pink) shows details that are invisible to humans. (See page 47 for a Web address where you can watch these pictures put together into a movie.)

Enhanced Color

Methane Band

23

FAR-OUT FACT

SPOTS OF MANY COLORS

Why did astronomers name Neptune's storm the Great Dark Spot? It is supposed to remind people of another famous storm: the Great Red Spot on Jupiter. Jupiter's Great Red Spot has been around for hundreds of years. It is a very long-lived storm! That is why scientists were so surprised when Neptune's Great Dark Spot disappeared. Apparently, not all great spots are the same. Different gas giants have different kinds of gigantic storms.

the weather on Earth better," explained Hammel. Each time astronomers look at Neptune, they see something different—a new bright spot or new storms. "Watching Neptune is like watching a work in progress," said Hammel. "You never know exactly what it's going to do next!"

NEPTUNE AT A GLANCE

Diameter: 49,528 kilometers (30,776 miles)

Volume: 58 Earths

Mass: 17 Earths, or 102,440,000,000,000 trillion kilograms

Position: Eighth planet from Sun

Average Distance from Sun: 4,498 million kilometers
   (2,795 million miles)

Day Length: 16 hours, 7 minutes

Year Length: 60,190 Earth days, or 165 Earth years

Color: Blue

Atmosphere: 79% hydrogen; 18% helium; 3% methane

Surface: None

Temperature: −214° Celsius (−353° Fahrenheit)

Moons: 13

Rings: 6

Namesake: Roman god of the sea

Symbol:

NEPTUNE

 ## Planet Fast Facts

★ Neptune is the farthest planet in our solar system. It is about 30 times as far from the Sun as Earth is.

★ Neptune receives about 900 times less sunlight than Earth.

★ Neptune was the first planet located through mathematical prediction, not observation.

★ Two men predicted Neptune's location: John Couch Adams and Urbain J.J. Le Verrier.

★ Johann Galle first observed Neptune in 1846 using a telescope and Le Verrier's predicted location.

★ Neptune is farther from the Sun than dwarf planet Pluto during part of its orbit.

★ There is no land on Neptune. It is made of a thick gaseous atmosphere with liquid underneath.

★ Methane, or natural gas, gives Neptune its blue color.

★ At more than 2,000 kilometers (1,200 miles) per hour, Neptune's winds are the fastest in the solar system.

★ Giant hurricane-like storms on Neptune come and go more quickly than those on Jupiter.

★ Neptune's weather is likely driven by heat deep inside it.

★ Neptune spins on a tilted axis, so it has seasons.

★ Ocean-colored Neptune was named after the Roman god of the sea.

★ Neptune is the smallest of the four gas giants.

★ Neptune is also called an ice giant, a type of large, cold, gaseous planet containing a lot of methane and ammonia.

★ In 2011, only one year, or a single orbit around the Sun, will have passed on Neptune since its discovery.

★ It takes nearly 165 Earth years for Neptune to travel once around the Sun.

★ Six uneven, faint, fading rings of dust and small rocks wrap around Neptune.

Neptune Moons Fast Facts

★ Neptune has 13 known moons: Triton, Nereid, Naiad, Thalassa, Despina, Galatea, Larissa, Proteus, Halimede, Psamathe, Sao, Laomedeia, and Neso. Their names come from sea gods and their relatives in Greek mythology.

★ Most of Neptune's moons are small, and there are likely more undiscovered small ones.

★ Triton is Neptune's biggest moon, by far. It is about 2,700 kilometers (1,680 miles) in diameter.

★ Triton is bigger than Pluto and nearly as big as Earth's moon.

★ Triton orbits in the opposite direction of Neptune's spin.

★ Triton probably did not form alongside Neptune. It was likely captured later by Neptune's gravity.

★ Triton is slowly getting closer to Neptune. In 10 million to 100 million years, Neptune's gravity will rip it apart. Triton's leftovers will likely become a ring system bigger than Saturn's.

★ With temperatures of −240°C (−400°F), Triton has the coldest temperatures ever measured in our solar system.

★ Icy volcanoes on Triton erupt cryolava.

★ Nereid has the most eccentric (long, thin, oval-shaped) orbit of any known moon.

★ Nereid's orbit is about seven times as far from Neptune at one end as at the other.

★ Triton's violent capture may have caused Nereid's odd orbit.

 ## Mission Fast Facts

★ Spaceships will never land on Neptune. There is no land.

★ No astronauts have traveled to Neptune. Only one flyby probe, *Voyager 2* in 1989, has visited the planet.

★ It took *Voyager 2* twelve years to reach Neptune.

★ *Voyager 2* studied Neptune's weather, including its Great Dark Spot.

★ *Voyager 2* discovered six of Neptune's moons.

Neptune Timeline
of Exploration and Discovery

1845 John Couch Adams predicts the location of Neptune based on Uranus's affected orbit.

1846 Urbain J.J. Le Verrier independently predicts the location of Neptune. Astronomer Johann Gottfried Galle uses Le Verrier's prediction to find Neptune with a telescope. William Lassell discovers the moon Triton.

1949 Gerard Kuiper discovers the moon Nereid.

1985 Astronomers discover rings around Neptune.

1989 *Voyager 2* becomes the first spacecraft to visit Neptune. It sends back 10,000 images of the planet, its moons, and ring system, including pictures of the Great Dark Spot. It discovers the moons Naiad, Thalassa, Despina, Galatea, Larissa, and Proteus.

1994–2005 *Hubble Space Telescope*, launched in 1990, observes Neptune's atmosphere and fast-changing weather.

2002–2003 Astronomers discover the moons Halimede, Psamathe, Sao, Laomedeia, and Neso using ground-based telescopes.

2007 Astronomers discover that Neptune's south pole is 10°C (18°F) hotter than the rest of the planet.

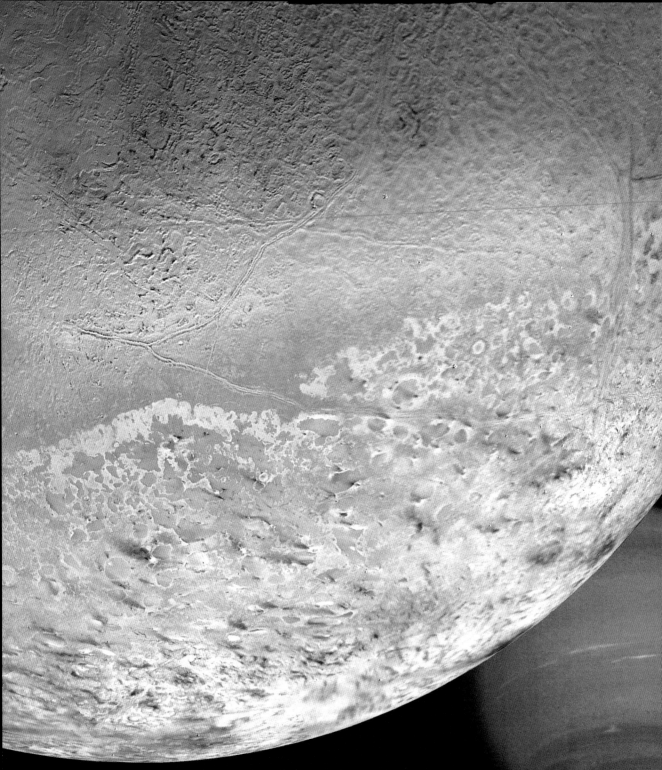

NEPTUNE'S largest moon, Triton, is an icy world.

CHAPTER 2

ODDBALL
TRITON

Neptune orbits on the edge of the solar system. But it is not alone out there. At least a dozen small moons keep Neptune company. And one big one! Triton is more than six times the size of any other moon of Neptune. It is about 2,700 kilometers (1,680 miles) across—three-quarters the size of Earth's large moon. Triton is even bigger than Pluto.

Triton is famous for more than being massive. It is a bizarre, backward world. All the other moons orbit around Neptune in the

THIRTEEN AND COUNTING . . .

An amateur astronomer discovered Triton. Englishman William Lassell spotted the moon just weeks after Neptune's discovery in 1846. A famous twentieth century astronomer, Gerard Kuiper, discovered a second moon more than 100 years later. He found Nereid in 1949. *Voyager 2* discovered six moons in 1989: Naiad, Thalassa, Despina, Galatea, Larissa, and Proteus. Astronomers armed with improved ground-based telescopes in 2002 and 2003 discovered five new small moons: Halimede, Psamathe, Sao, Laomedeia, and Neso.

ASTRONOMERS using a telescope in Chile discovered this moon of Neptune in 2002. It was later named Halimede.

same direction that Neptune spins. Triton circles Neptune in the opposite direction! This is called a retrograde orbit. It is rare in our solar system. Triton is the only known large retrograde moon.

VOYAGE TO TRITON

Voyager 2 taught us most of what we know about Triton. It made many discoveries, including a thin atmosphere of nitrogen gas around Triton. (Saturn's moon Titan and Earth are the only other known worlds with a lot of nitrogen in their atmospheres.) *Voyager 2* photographed Triton's odd surface, too. One side looks like cantaloupe skin. The other side is full of rugged valleys and ridges.

All of Triton is icy. The ice reflects nearly all of what little sunlight reaches it. This makes for the coldest temperatures ever measured in the solar system. Triton is –240 degrees Celsius (–400 degrees Fahrenheit)! Even the volcanoes on Triton are frozen. *Voyager 2* photographed ice volcanoes on Triton. The images amazed astronomers. Volcanoes on Earth erupt melted rock, or lava. Ice volcanoes spew out icy frozen lava called cryolava. Triton's cryolava is a probably a mixture of liquid nitrogen,

VOYAGER 2 took this picture of Triton on August 24, 1989, from about 530,000 kilometers (330,000 miles) away.

LOOK for the many dark streaks on this *Voyager 2* picture. They are plumes of cryolava erupting from ice volcanoes on Triton.

dust, and frozen methane. When an ice volcano erupts, cryolava shoots up into the air. It then instantly freezes and falls—as snow!

SWITCHING PARTNERS

Voyager 2 did leave some of Triton's mysteries unsolved, like where it came from. Triton did not form alongside Neptune. How do scientists know that? Because Triton's

FAR-OUT FACT

WHERE DO MOONS COME FROM?

Most big moons formed alongside their parent planet. They are leftover chunks from when the planet clumped into being. Jupiter's moons Io, Europa, Ganymede, and Callisto are good examples of big moons that formed this way. They formed from the same cloud of dust and gas as Jupiter. Small moons are different. Many were once asteroids, comets, or other objects until a planet's gravity grabbed them. Once captured, they began orbiting and became moons. Mars's potato-shaped moons Deimos and Phobos are small moons that were once asteroids.

retrograde orbit takes it the wrong way! If Triton formed alongside Neptune, both worlds would move in the same direction. Astronomers think Triton formed somewhere else, then Neptune's powerful gravity captured it later.

Neptune capturing Triton is easier said than done. Remember, Triton is really big—too big for Neptune's gravity to simply pluck it from its own path around the Sun. But if Triton had slowed down, then Neptune could have captured it. What could slow down something that big? "In Triton's case, something that's not there now had to be there then," said astronomer Craig Agnor. Agnor and fellow astronomer Douglas Hamilton think they know what might be missing: Triton's double. The scientists think that Triton once orbited the Sun with a partner. The two were a binary system, or "double planet." They circled each other as both orbited the Sun together. (Pluto and its big moon Charon are another binary system.)

What happened to Triton and its partner? Agnor and Hamilton think that maybe billions of years ago, Triton and its partner passed too close to Neptune. Neptune's gravity separated them and the partner was flung away.

Triton

TRITON and its binary partner get dangerously close to Neptune in this illustration.

VOYAGER 2 took this grainy picture of Neptune's rings in 1989.

FAR-OUT FACT

RINGS OF CHANGE

Neptune has rings as well as moons. About six thin, faint, dark rings circle the farthest planet. The rings are made of dust and small rocks. Neptune's rings are hard to see. They are uneven and clumpy, and some sections of the rings are thicker and brighter than others. Keck telescope pictures from 2002–2003 show that the rings have faded since *Voyager 2* was there. Astronomers do not know why Neptune's rings are uneven, nor do they know why they are fading.

Losing its partner slowed Triton down. Neptune caught the slowing Triton, capturing it as its biggest moon.

Triton's future will be as action-packed as its past. Moving against the flow of your parent planet causes problems. Triton's retrograde orbit will eventually destroy the moon. Moving against Neptune's spin saps Triton's energy. Every year Triton slows a tiny bit—and drops closer to Neptune. Eventually Triton will get too close, and Neptune's gravity will break the moon apart. When will this happen? Not any time too soon—Triton still has a few million years left.

CHAPTER 3

WHAT'S NEXT FOR NEPTUNE?

Neptune is still keeping secrets. What do scientists still want to know? They have a long list! Neptune changes so much, and so fast. A year on Neptune lasts nearly 165 Earth years. We have only had the tools to watch its weather for weeks in Neptune time. So who can say what seasons on Neptune are like, or if storms are common? And how can such a sunless planet even have weather?

THE Keck I telescope on top of Hawaii's Mauna Kea has its dome open and is ready to watch the sky. It has taken some awesome pictures of Neptune.

A CLEARER VIEW

No space probe will deliver answers any time soon. Even if one left Earth today, it would take a decade to get to Neptune. The next possible spacecraft mission to Neptune will not leave before 2019. Meanwhile, astronomers will keep studying Neptune with telescopes. The *Hubble* has taught us a lot about the planet, but the orbiting space telescope will not last forever. It will likely quit working around 2014.

FAR-OUT FACT

GOING BACK TO NEPTUNE

What is the next hoped-for space mission to Neptune? It is a flyby space probe called *Argo*. Astronomer and Neptune expert Heidi Hammel is trying to get **NASA** to take on the mission. These days, space probe missions compete for money from **NASA**. If *Argo* is chosen, its earliest possible launch date is not until 2019. So the spacecraft's design is not decided yet. *Argo* would study Neptune and also Triton after an eight-year journey from Earth.

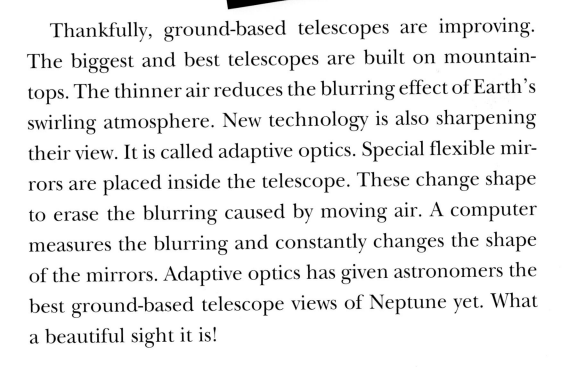

Thankfully, ground-based telescopes are improving. The biggest and best telescopes are built on mountain-tops. The thinner air reduces the blurring effect of Earth's swirling atmosphere. New technology is also sharpening their view. It is called adaptive optics. Special flexible mirrors are placed inside the telescope. These change shape to erase the blurring caused by moving air. A computer measures the blurring and constantly changes the shape of the mirrors. Adaptive optics has given astronomers the best ground-based telescope views of Neptune yet. What a beautiful sight it is!

Words to Know

adaptive optics—Telescope technology that lessens the blurring effects of light traveling through the atmosphere.

asteroid—A large rock, smaller than a planet or dwarf planet, that orbits the Sun.

astronomer—A scientist who studies moons, stars, planets, and the universe.

atmosphere—The gases that are held by gravity around a planet, moon, or other object in space.

binary system—Two objects in space that orbit each other.

comet—A large chunk of frozen gases, ice, and dust that orbits the Sun.

core—The center, usually solid, of a planet or moon.

cryolava—Frozen icy material that erupts from an ice volcano, or cryovolcano.

dwarf planet—A round space object that orbits the Sun and may orbit with other objects.

flyby probe—A space probe that flies by a planet or moon.

gas giant—A planet made of mostly gas and liquid and no land, including Jupiter, Saturn, Uranus, and Neptune.

gravity—An attractive force on one object from another.

ground-based telescope—A telescope on Earth.

lava—Melted rock that comes out of a volcano.

mass—The amount of matter in something.

methane—A gas made of a combination of carbon and hydrogen.

moon—An object in space that naturally orbits a larger object in space.

NASA—The National Aeronautics and Space Administration, the space agency of the United States.

orbit—The path followed by a planet, moon, or other object around another object in space; to move around an object in space.

orbiter—A space probe that orbits a planet, moon, or other object in space.

planet—A large object in space that is alone in its orbit around the Sun.

planetary astronomer—An astronomer who studies planets and moons.

retrograde orbit—An orbit in the opposite direction from the orbit of most of the planets and moons in a solar system.

solar system—A sun and everything that orbits it.

space probe—A robotic spacecraft launched into space to collect information.

space telescope—A telescope that orbits Earth or travels in space.

sun—The star in the center of a solar system.

volcano—A break in a planet or moon's surface where melted rock and gas can escape.

volume—The amount of space something fills.

weight—The force of gravity on a mass.

Find Out More and Get Updates

Books

Bortz, Fred. *Beyond Jupiter: The Story of Planetary Astronomer Heidi Hammel.* Washington, D.C.: Joseph Henry Press, 2005.

Bourgeois, Paulette. *The Jumbo Book of Space.* Toronto: Kids Can Press, 2007.

Carruthers, Margaret. *The Hubble Space Telescope.* New York: Franklin Watts, 2003.

Carson, Mary Kay. *Exploring the Solar System: A History with 22 Activities.* Chicago: Chicago Review Press, 2008.

Miller, Ron. *Uranus and Neptune.* Brookfield, Conn.: Twenty-First Century Books, 2003.

Tabak, John. *A Look at Neptune.* New York: Franklin Watts, 2003.

Solar System Web Sites

Solar System Exploration
<http://solarsystem.nasa.gov/kids>
Neptune's Moons
<http://www.kidsastronomy.com/neptune/
    moons.htm>

Neptune Mission Web Sites

The Hubble Space Telescope

<http://hubblesite.org>

The Voyager Missions
<http://spaceplace.nasa.gov/en/kids/vgr_fact3.shtml>

Planet-watching Web Sites

NightSky Sky Calendar
<http://www.space.com/spacewatch/sky_calendar.html>

StarDate Online: Solar System Guide:
<http://stardate.org/resources/ssguide/neptune.html>

Neptune Movie

Watch the 39-second movie made from *Hubble*'s 2005 images.
<http://hubblesite.org/newscenter/archive/releases/2005/22/
    video>

Index

A

Adams, John Couch, 9
Agnor, Craig, 36
Argo, 42

C

cryolava, 33, 35

D

Discovery, 18

E

Earth, 16, 18, 20, 21, 24, 33, 40

G

Galle, Johann, 9
Great Dark Spot, 18, 20, 21, 24
Great Red Spot, 24

H

Hammel, Heidi, 10, 12, 14, 16, 20, 21, 24, 42
Hamilton, Douglas, 36
Herschel, William, 8
Hubble Space Telescope, 18, 21, 42

J

Jupiter, 7, 8, 14, 16, 24, 35

K

Kuiper, Gerard, 32

L

Lassell, William, 32
Le Verrier, Urbain J.J., 9

M

Mars, 8, 35
Mercury, 8
methane, 7, 35
moons, 16, 31, 32, 35
  Triton, *see* Triton

N

Neptune
  atmosphere, 16, 20
  clouds, 14, 18
  color, 7
  composition, 7
  discovery, 8–9, 10
  distance from Sun, 5
  moons, 16, 31, 32, 35
  name, 9
  rings, 5, 16, 38

  weather, 7, 14, 16, 18, 20, 21, 24, 40

P

Pluto, 6, 36

S

Saturn, 5, 7, 8, 14, 16

T

Triton
  atmosphere, 33
  capture by Neptune, 35–36, 39
  composition, 33
  destruction, 39
  discovery, 32
  ice volcanoes, 33, 35
  orbit, 31, 33, 35–36
  size, 31

U

Uranus, 7, 8, 9, 14, 16

V

Venus, 8
Voyager 1, 14
Voyager 2, 14, 16, 18, 21, 32, 33, 35, 38